BIOGRAPHIES FOR KIDS
ALL ABOUT ANNE FRANK

WHO WAS SHE?

CHILDREN'S BIOGRAPHIES OF FAMOUS PEOPLE BOOKS

BABY PROFESSOR

EDUCATION KIDS

Speedy Publishing LLC
40 E. Main St. #1156
Newark, DE 19711
www.speedypublishing.com

Copyright 2016

All about Anne Frank.

Who Was She?

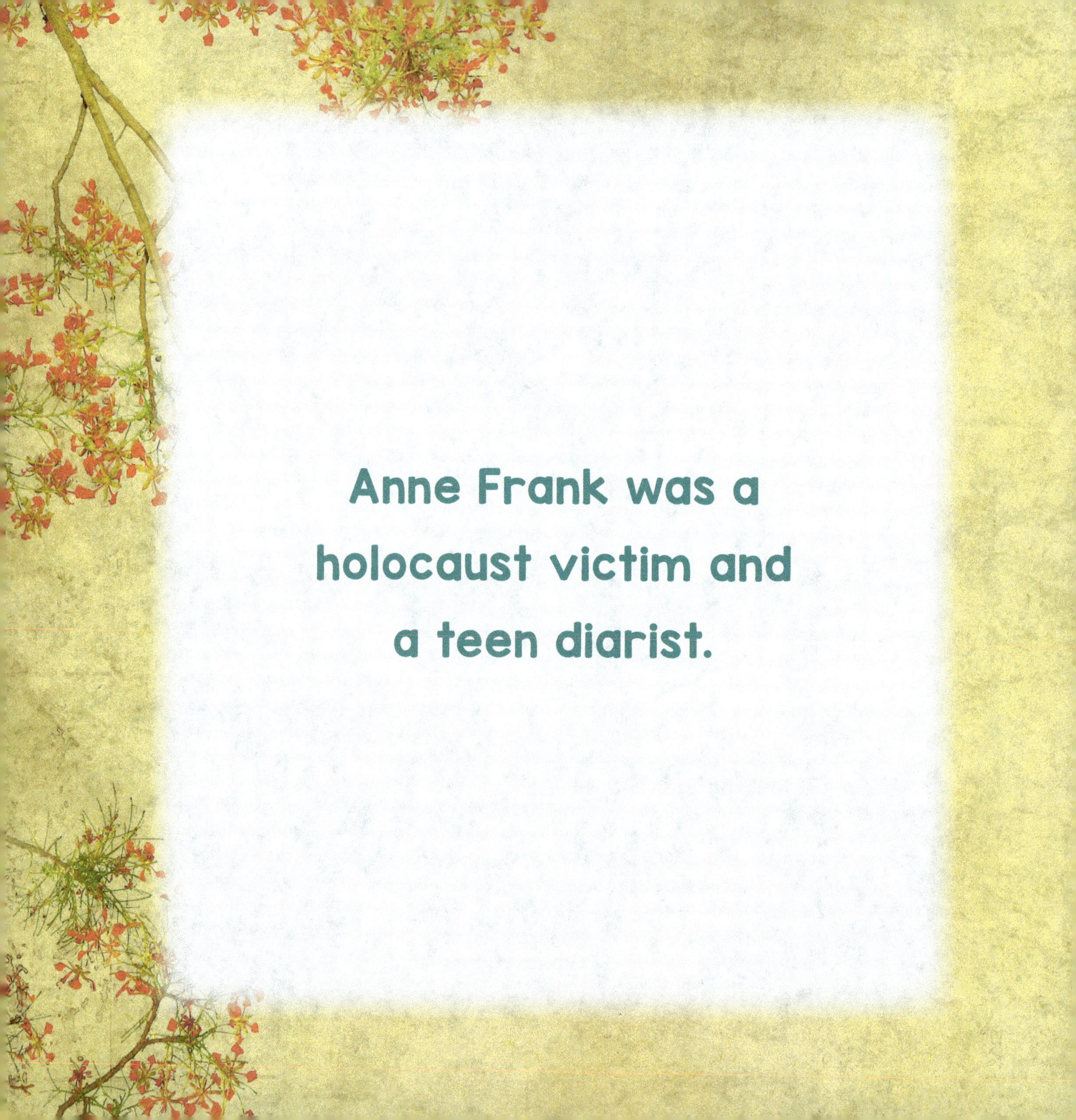

Anne Frank was a
holocaust victim and
a teen diarist.

Let's get to know Anne Frank!

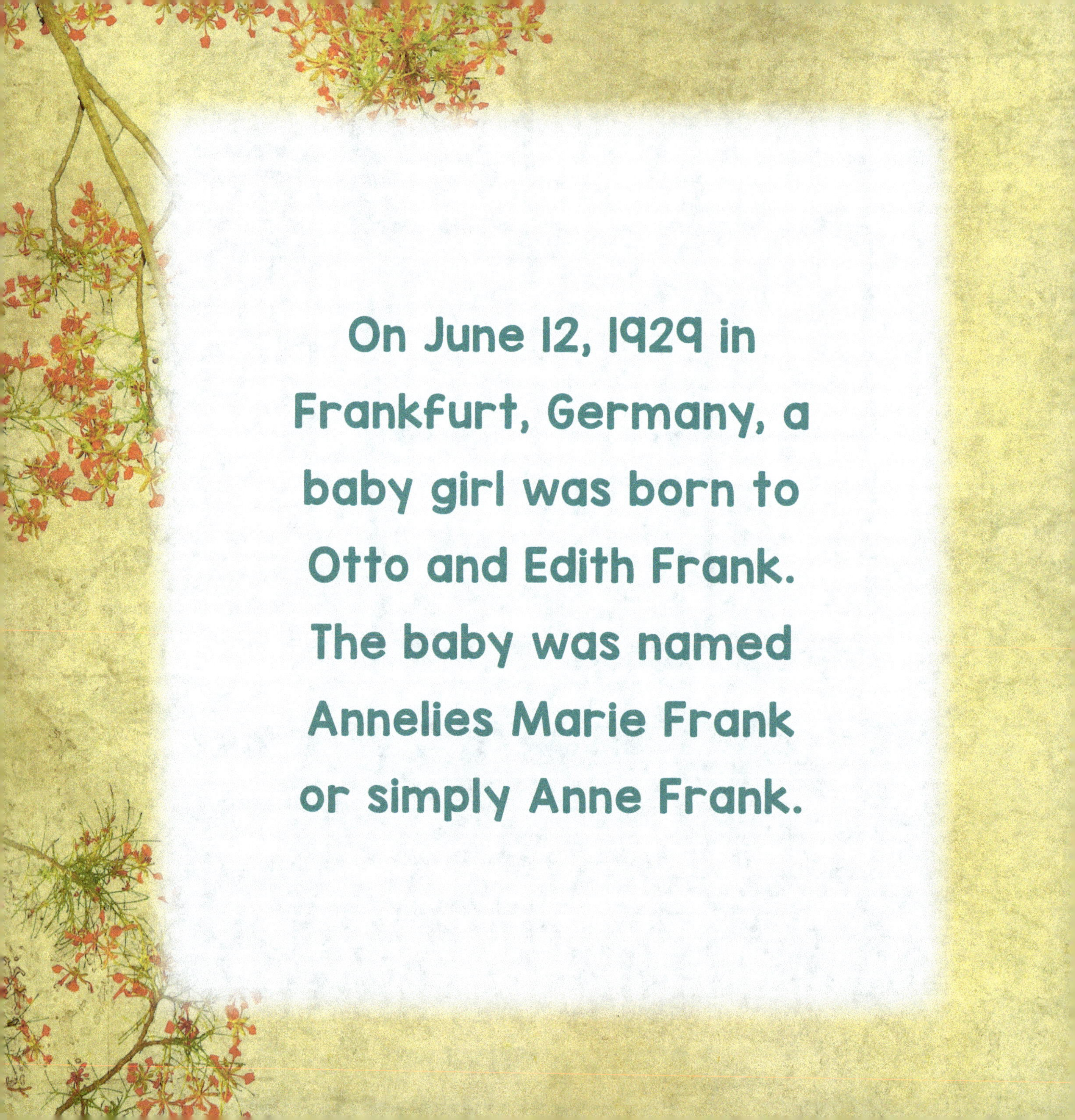
On June 12, 1929 in
Frankfurt, Germany, a
baby girl was born to
Otto and Edith Frank.
The baby was named
Annelies Marie Frank
or simply Anne Frank.

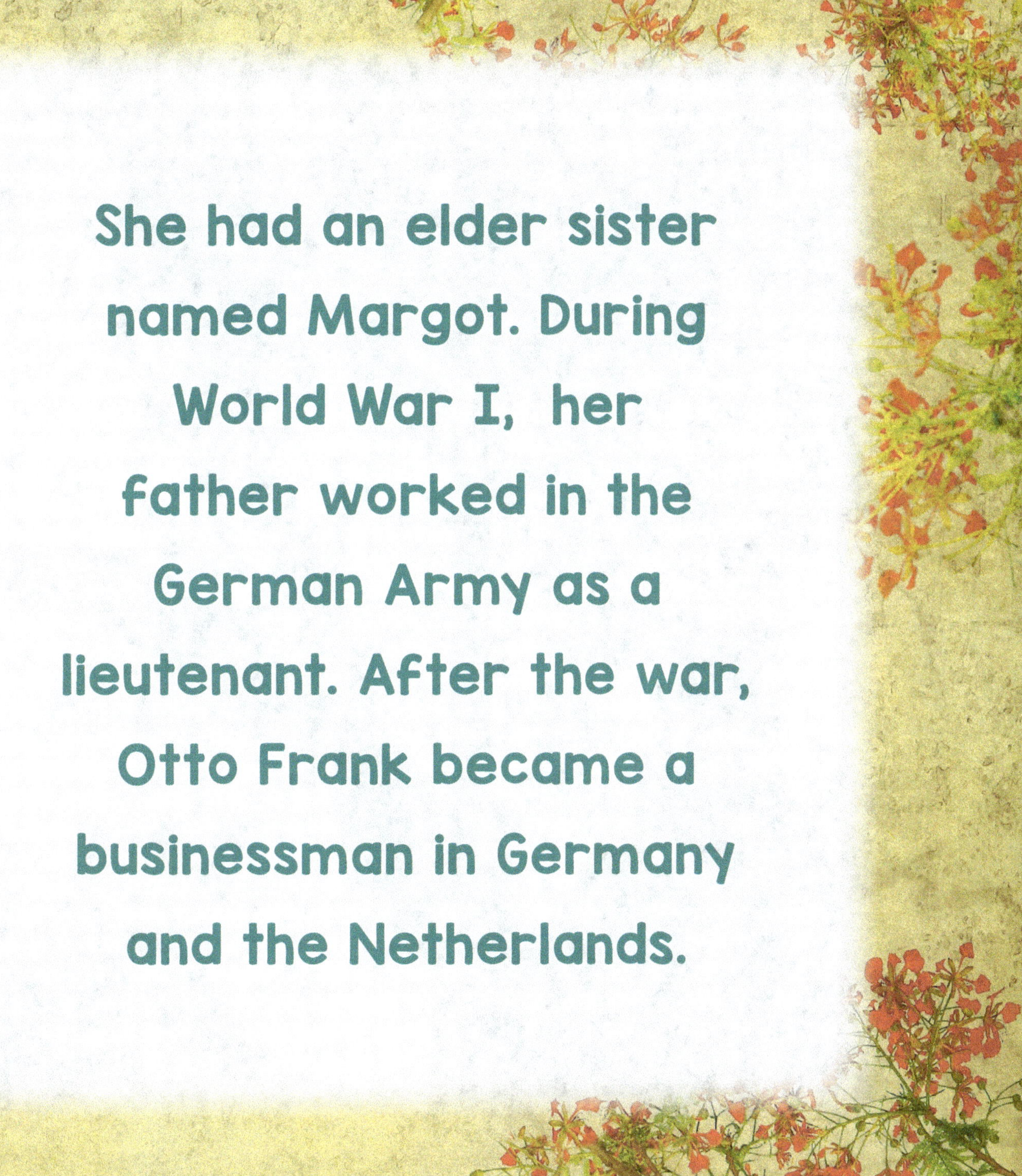

She had an elder sister named Margot. During World War I, her father worked in the German Army as a lieutenant. After the war, Otto Frank became a businessman in Germany and the Netherlands.

In 1934, Anne Frank
attended Amsterdam's
Sixth Montessori School.

Anne had many friends
and had enjoyed
normal childhood life.

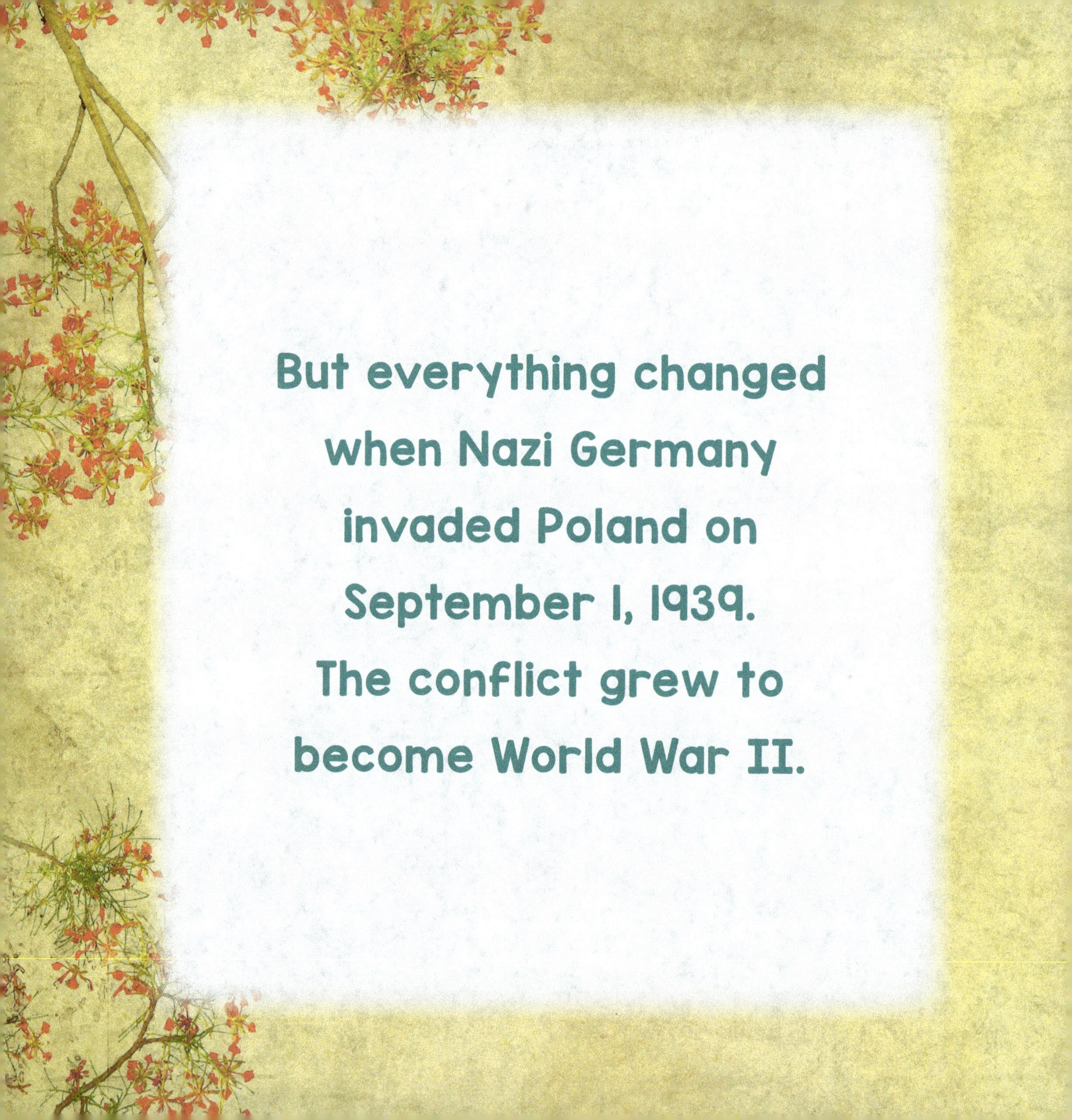

But everything changed
when Nazi Germany
invaded Poland on
September 1, 1939.
The conflict grew to
become World War II.

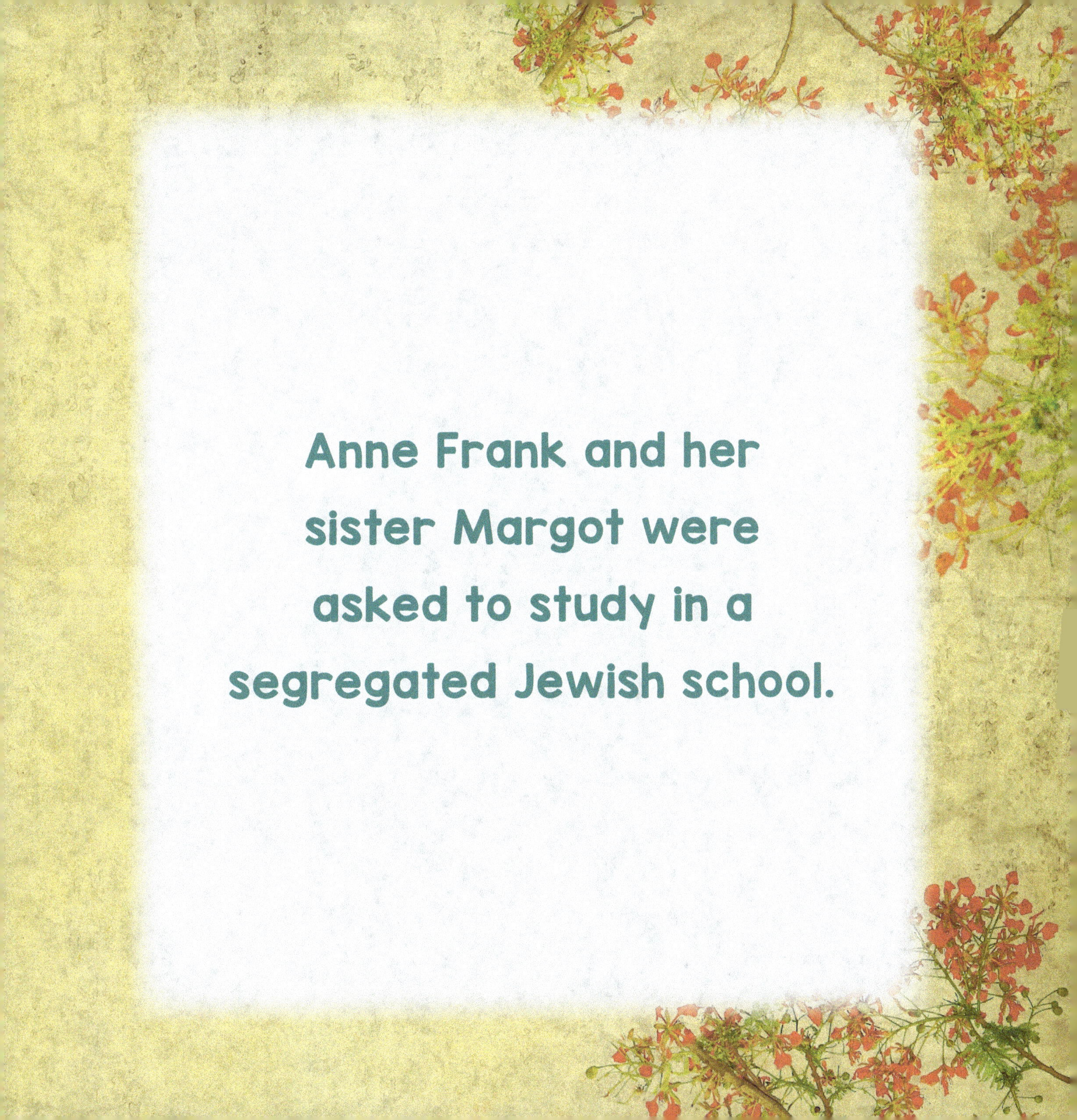

Anne Frank and her sister Margot were asked to study in a segregated Jewish school.

Anne Franks house
in Amsterdam.

On her 13th birthday,
Anne received a precious
gift from her parents,
a red checked diary.

Anne Frank used the name Kitty as her imaginary friend in her diary entries.

View of the Prinsengracht and the House of Anne Frank in Amsterdam.

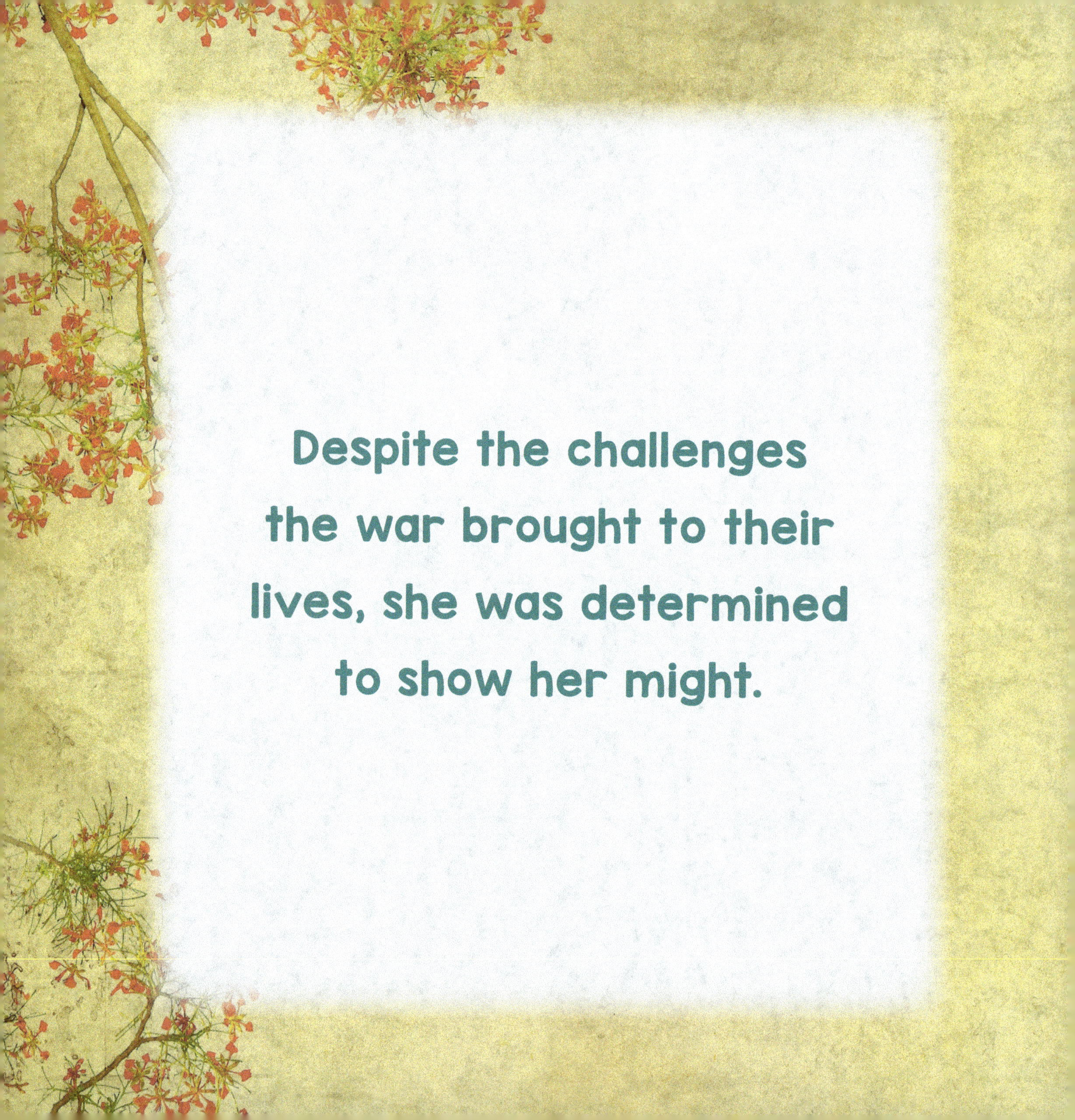

Despite the challenges
the war brought to their
lives, she was determined
to show her might.

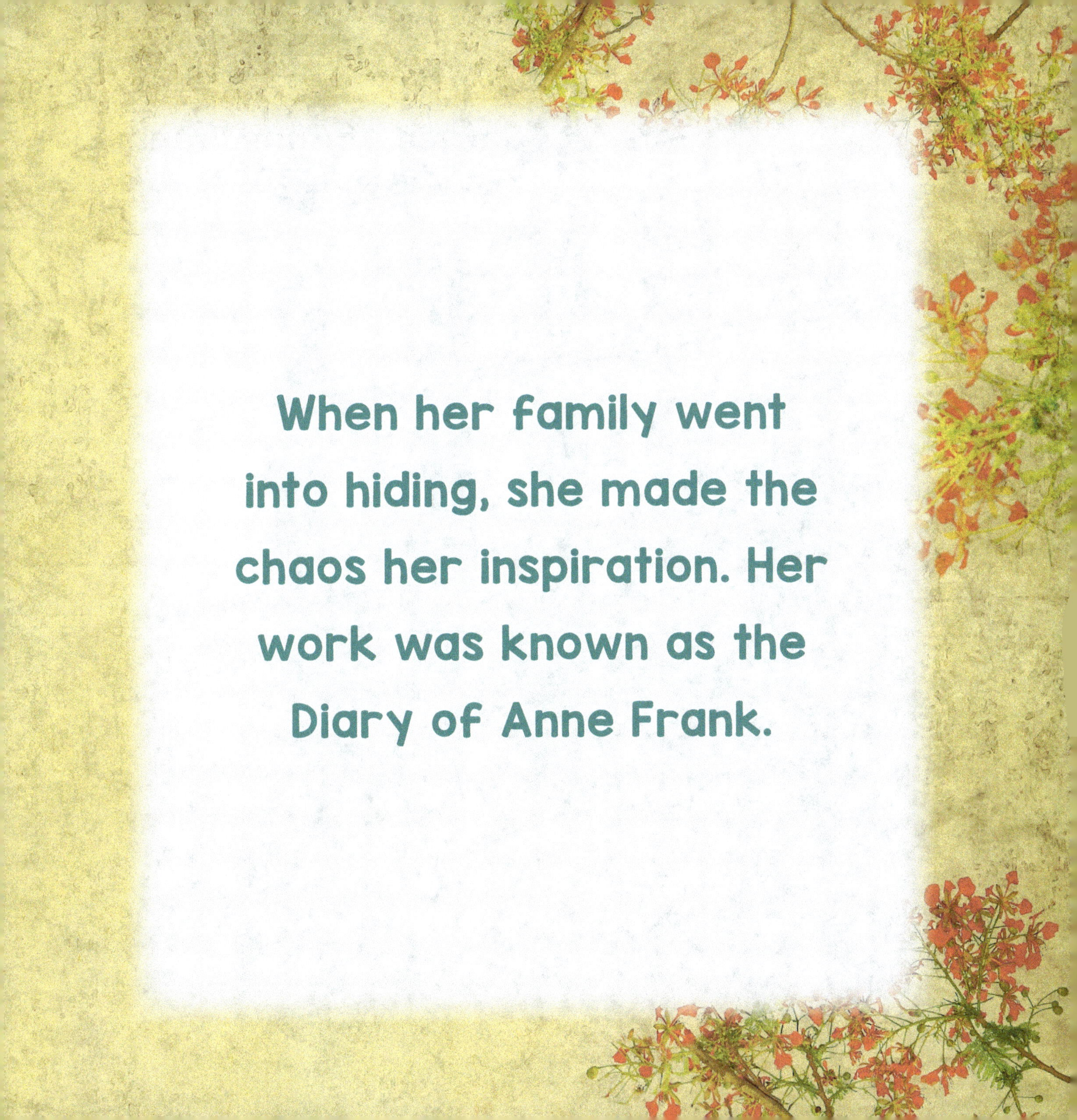

When her family went into hiding, she made the chaos her inspiration. Her work was known as the Diary of Anne Frank.

Garden of Anne Frank.
Paris, France.

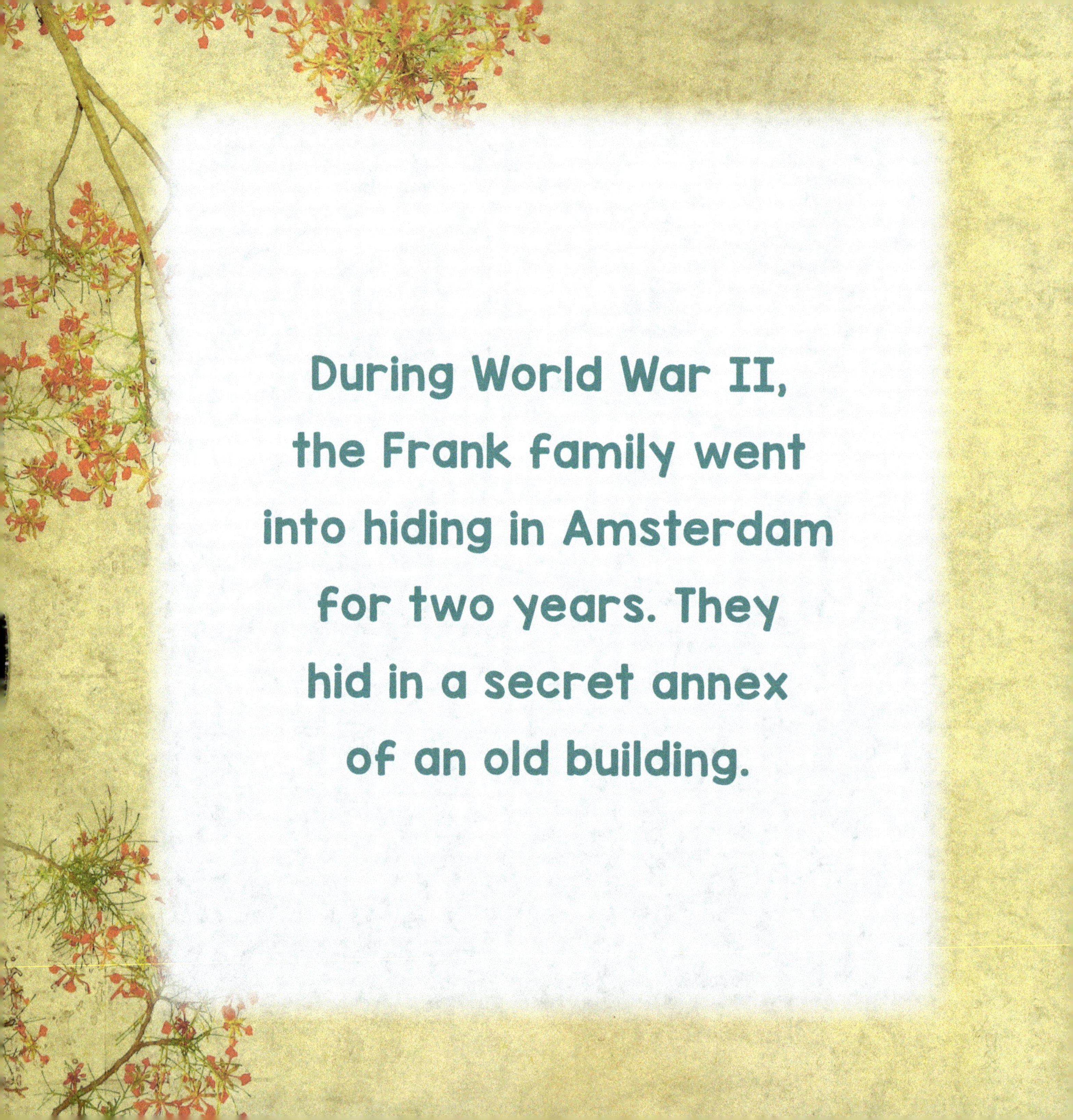
During World War II,
the Frank family went
into hiding in Amsterdam
for two years. They
hid in a secret annex
of an old building.

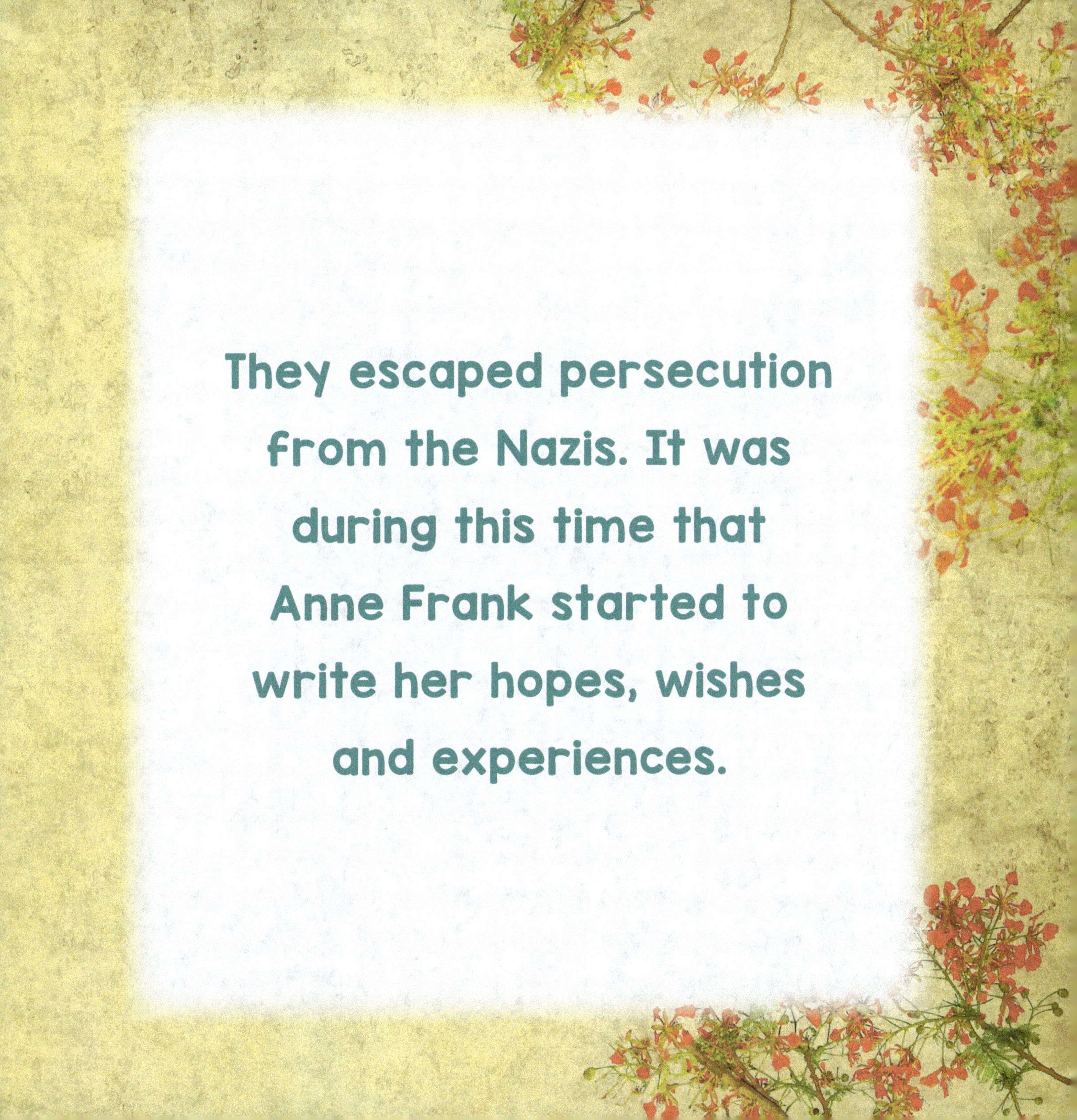

They escaped persecution from the Nazis. It was during this time that Anne Frank started to write her hopes, wishes and experiences.

Garden of Anne Frank.
Paris, France.

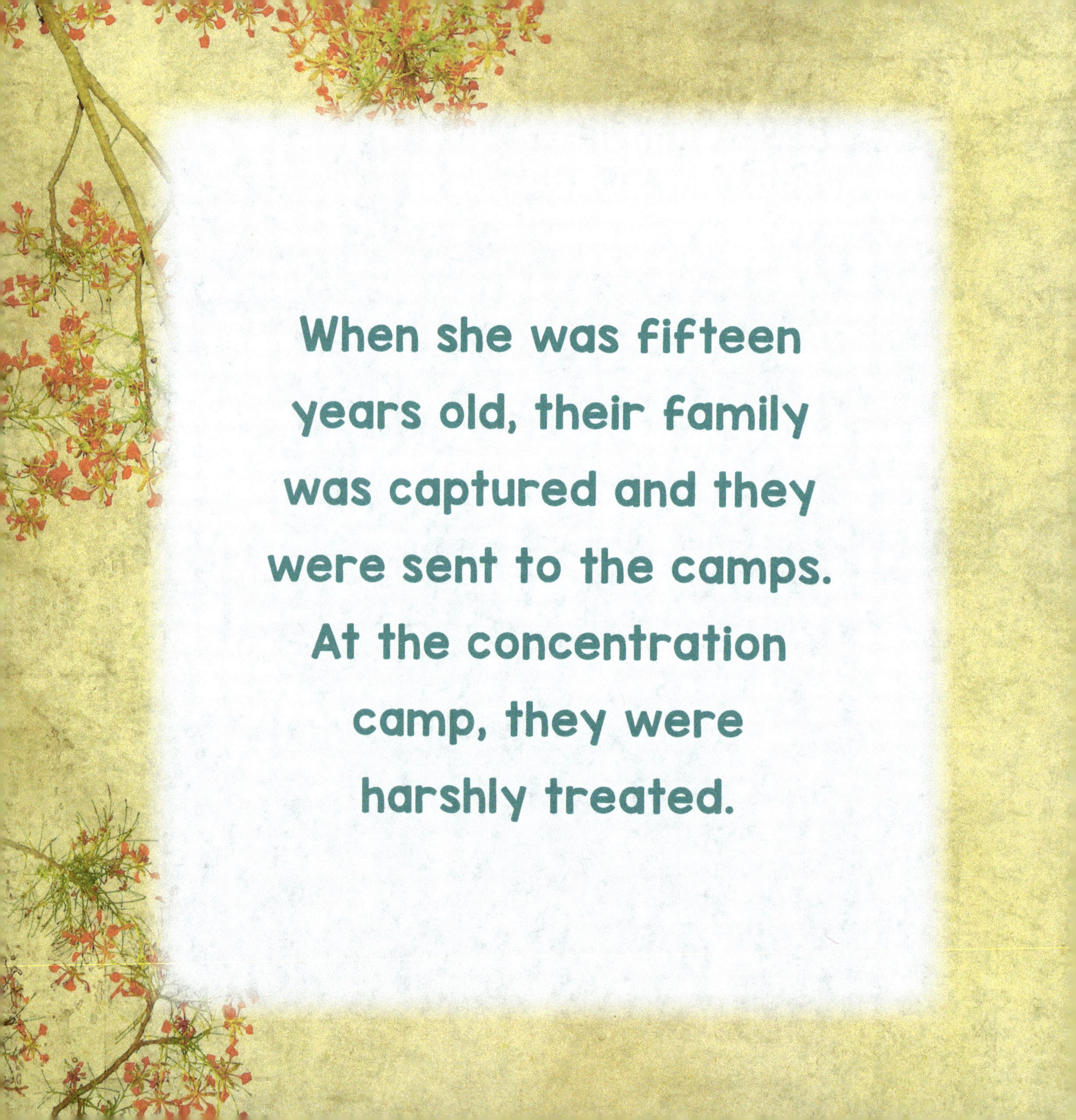

When she was fifteen
years old, their family
was captured and they
were sent to the camps.
At the concentration
camp, they were
harshly treated.

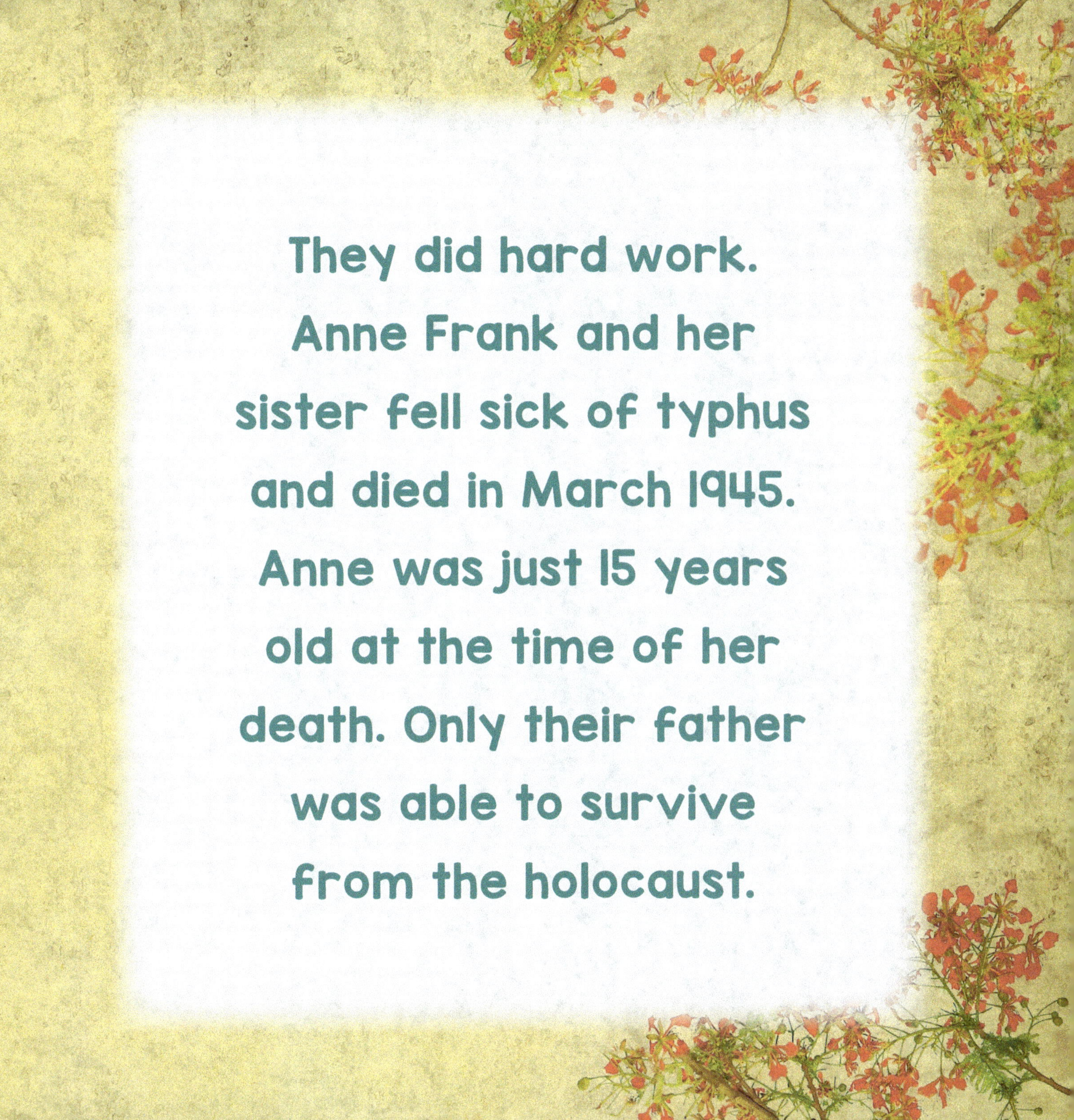

They did hard work.
Anne Frank and her
sister fell sick of typhus
and died in March 1945.
Anne was just 15 years
old at the time of her
death. Only their father
was able to survive
from the holocaust.

"I
I still bel

ite of everything,
e that people are good."
Anne Frank

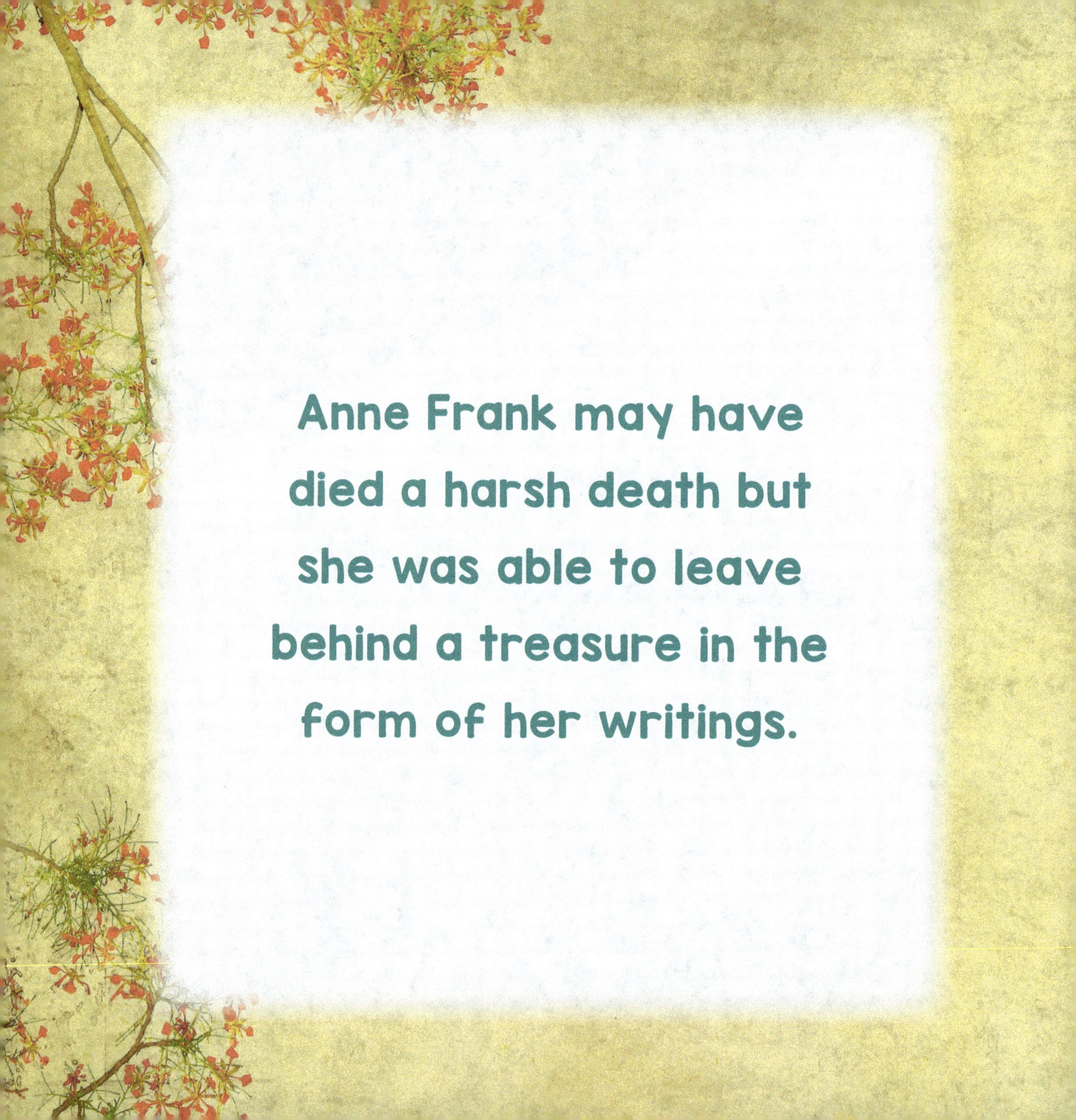

Anne Frank may have died a harsh death but she was able to leave behind a treasure in the form of her writings.

Don't you just love the
bravery and spirit of
this young teen diarist?

Visit

BABY PROFESSOR
EDUCATION KIDS

www.BabyProfessorBooks.com
to download Free Baby Professor eBooks
and view our catalog of new and exciting
Children's Books